THE NILE RIVER
THE LONGEST RIVER

Aileen Weintraub

The Rosen Publishing Group's
PowerKids Press™
New York

Published in 2001 by The Rosen Publishing Group, Inc.
29 East 21st Street, New York, NY 10010

First Edition

Book Design: Michael J. Caroleo
Illustration on page 4 by Michael J. Caroleo

Photo Credits: Cover (Great Pyramids) and p. 19 © Christian Michaels/FPG; cover (painting) © Historical Picture Archive/CORBIS; background image on all pages © TRAVELPIX/FPG; pp. 7, 12, 15, 16 © National Geographic; p. 8 © Chinch Gryniewicz, Ecoscene/CORBIS; p. 11 © David Bartruff/FPG; p. 19 (camels) © Fergus O'Brien/FPG; p. 20 (Aswan Dam) © Lloyd Clufff/CORBIS; p. 20 (Lake Nasser) © Gian Berto Vanni/CORBIS.

Weintraub, Aileen, 1973–
      The Nile, the longest river / Aileen Weintraub.— 1st ed.
        p. cm.—(Great record breakers in nature)
      Includes index.
      Summary: Describes the location, climate, history, and importance of the Nile, the longest river in the world.
      ISBN 0-8239-5638-5 (alk. paper)
      1. Nile River—History—Juvenile literature. [1.Nile River.] I. Title. II. Series.

DT115 .W388 2000
962—dc21   00-023908

Manufactured in the United States of America

CONTENTS

1	A Long and Winding River	5
2	White Nile, Blue Nile	6
3	A Great Mystery Solved	9
4	Partly Sunny, Partly Cloudy	10
5	Water, Water Everywhere	13
6	The Nile Creates a Nation	14
7	The Ancient River	17
8	Life on the Nile	18
9	The High Aswan Dam	21
10	The Gift of the Nile	22
	Glossary	23
	Index	24
	Web Sites	24

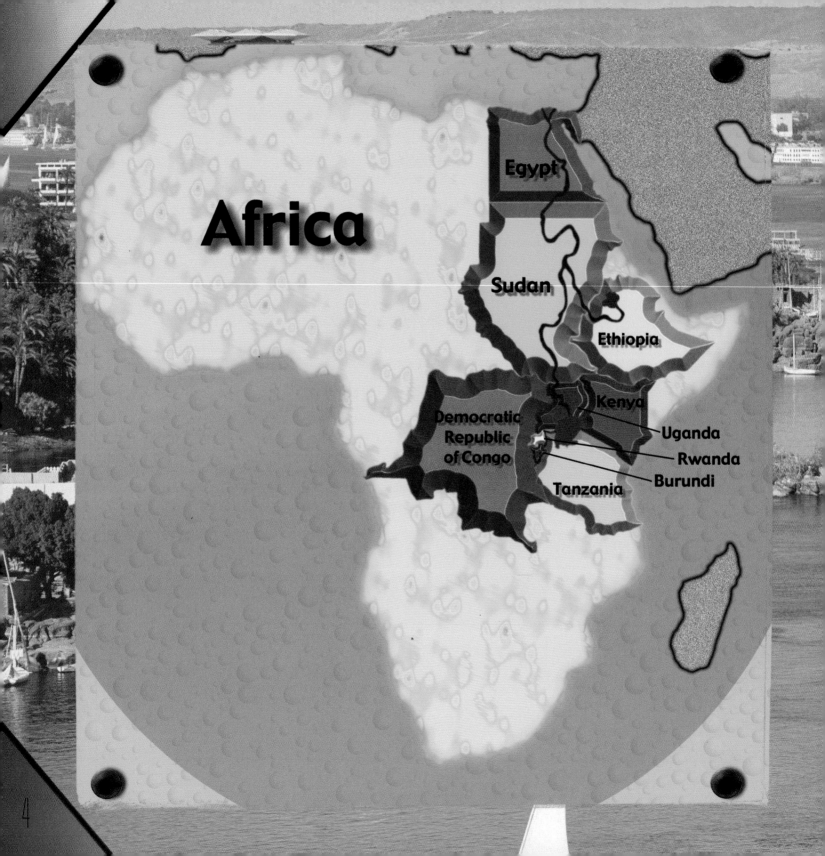

Africa

Egypt

Sudan

Ethiopia

Kenya

Democratic
Republic
of Congo

Uganda

Rwanda

Burundi

Tanzania

4

A LONG AND WINDING RIVER

Imagine yourself flying in an airplane. When you look down at the ground, you see a long green ribbon twisting endlessly. On either side of the ribbon is dry desert land. This is what the Nile River looks like from the sky. The Nile is the longest river in the world. It is located on the continent of Africa. The Nile is 4,160 miles (6,695 km) long. It is so long that it runs through nine different countries in Africa. It is an unusual river because it flows from south to north. Most rivers flow from north to south. Scientists believe that the Nile is over 30 million years old.

◀ *The Nile runs through nine different countries. These countries are Tanzania, Burundi, Rwanda, Democratic Republic of Congo, Uganda, Kenya, Ethiopia, Sudan, and Egypt.*

WHITE NILE, BLUE NILE

The White Nile and the Blue Nile are the two main **tributaries** of the Nile River. The Blue Nile is shorter than the White Nile, but it is more powerful because it has much more water. About 70 percent of the Nile's water comes from the Blue Nile. The Blue Nile begins in the **highlands** of a country called Ethiopia. The White Nile begins as the Kagera River in the highlands of a country called Uganda. The Blue Nile and White Nile travel separately until they meet in the country of Sudan. As a single river, the water then flows north to the Mediterranean Sea. The Nile's average flow of water is 818,933 gallons (3.1 million liters) per second.

The Blue Nile and the White Nile meet in Kharthoum, Sudan. ▶

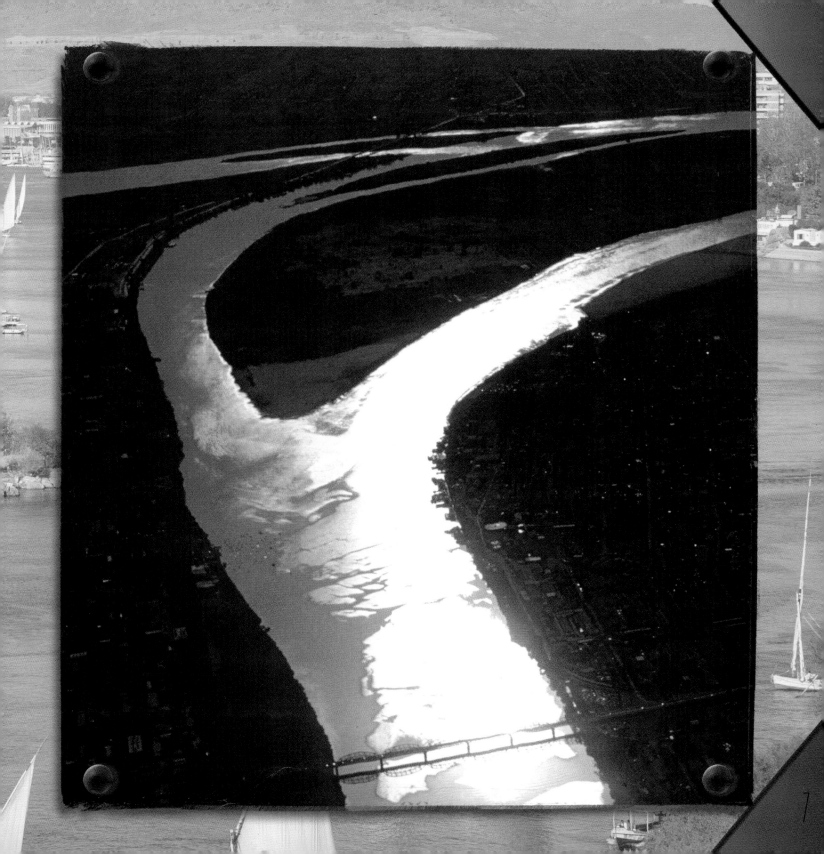

A GREAT MYSTERY SOLVED

For hundreds of years, no one knew where the Nile came from. It was one of the greatest mysteries on Earth. The **origin** of the Blue Nile was discovered in 1618 by a Spanish priest named Pedro Páez. The Blue Nile's origin is a spring in the Ethiopian highlands. From there it flows into Lake Tana, which is also in the Ethiopian highlands. In 1889, an explorer named Sir Henry Morton Stanley reached Lake Edward and the Ruwenzori mountains. Stanley had finally solved the rest of the mystery. The origin of the White Nile was in the Ruwenzori mountains in Uganda.

The Nile flows through many lakes, including Lake Victoria. This lake is the second largest freshwater lake in the world. Lake Victoria is a major source of the Nile.

PARTLY SUNNY, PARTLY CLOUDY

The Nile River runs through hot desert land. In some areas, temperatures can rise above 120 degrees **Fahrenheit** (49 degrees C). The people living along the Nile think of it as an important source of life. If it weren't for the water from the Nile, people would not be able to survive in this region. The Nile and the lands around it experience two very different types of **climate** during the summer. The northern part of the Nile has hardly any rainfall. However, Ethiopia, in the south, has very heavy rain during the summer. This heavy summer rain is very important because the hot weather slowly dries up the Nile. The river is at its lowest point between March and May. The Nile needs this rain to fill it up and to help keep it flowing.

People who live in the desert depend on the Nile for many things. These men are using mud from the Nile to make bricks. ▶

WATER, WATER EVERYWHERE

Some people believe that the Nile has a life of its own. In some places, the river is calm and quiet. In other places, there are rocky waterfalls, deep unexpected drops, and raging rapids. Long ago when the summer rains came, the Nile would rise so high that it would flood the land. The flooding left thick, black mud. This mud was rich in **minerals**. These minerals helped crops grow. Slowly, people began settling along the Nile. They realized that the summer floods were good for the land.

Cairo, Egypt, is one of the main cities along the Nile. Some parts of the Nile have calm waters, while other areas have waterfalls and rapids.

THE NILE CREATES A NATION

Thousands of years ago, people began building houses made of mud bricks along the banks of the Nile. Sometimes these houses fell apart during the floods. At this time Egypt was divided into two lands called Upper and Lower Egypt. The people from Upper and Lower Egypt often fought each other for power and land. Around 2925 B.C., Upper Egypt finally **conquered** Lower Egypt. The people from Upper and Lower Egypt realized that if they helped each other control the floods instead of fighting, life would be easier. The two lands joined together under King Menes. The Nile was an important reason why one of the first nations in the history of the world was created.

King Menes set up his kingdom along the banks of the Nile. He is famous for being the first king of the nation of Egypt. ▶

THE ANCIENT RIVER

Irrigation was first practiced in Egypt almost 5,000 years ago. The people would wait until the floods came. Then they would use this water to help grow their crops. The **ancient** Egyptians made one of the world's first calendars. This allowed them to keep track of the floods. Their calendar let them know how much time they had to prepare the land before the floods came. Priests measured how much the Nile rose by using stone columns that we now call nilometers. If the Nile rose too much, it would cause a flood and destroy the land. If the river didn't rise enough, this would mean that there wouldn't be enough water for crops. If this happened, people might starve.

◄ *The Nile is a source of life for many people. These farmers are picking lettuce from their field, which is watered by the Nile.*

LIFE ON THE NILE

Life in ancient Egypt centered around the Nile. Animals that lived in and along the river, such as camels, birds, fish, and even crocodiles, were used for food. Other animals were **worshiped** as gods. Boats were built to help with trade and war. The Egyptians also built monuments along the Nile. They carried **limestone** across the river to build the great **pyramids**. The pyramids are among the oldest monuments in the world. People still wonder how they were built. The Nile had its own god named Hapi, Lord of Fishes. Many Egyptians believed that Hapi had a water jar. If he did not tilt the jar enough, there would be a **drought**. The Egyptians prayed to Hapi to tilt the jar just right so they would have enough water.

This picture shows two people leading camels past the great pyramids. No one is sure exactly how these monuments were made. ▶

THE HIGH ASWAN DAM

The ancient Egyptians built high walls to keep the floodwaters from destroying their houses. Today things are different. The High Aswan Dam prevents homes and crops from being destroyed by flooding. The dam was completed in 1970, after 10 years of work. It cost over one billion dollars to build. The dam rises 364 feet (111 m) above the Nile River and is 12,562 feet (3,829 m) long. The floodwater from the Nile is now stored in an **artificial** lake that was built to hold the water. This lake, called Lake Nasser, stretches over 300 miles (483 km). Lake Nasser does more than stop flooding. It also provides Egyptians with enough water to last them throughout the year.

◀ *This is a picture of the High Aswan Dam. The Nile River irrigates 6 million acres (24,281 sq km) of land in Egypt. Some of the best farming areas in the world are along the Nile.*

THE GIFT OF THE NILE

An ancient **historian** named Herodotus once called Egypt the "gift of the Nile." This is because the Nile is very important to the lives of so many people. More than 40 million Egyptians depend on the Nile for survival. The Nile is an exciting, magical place. People worship by the banks of the Nile. Statues have been built and songs have been written to honor this ancient river. Artists come from all over the world to paint it. There is an old **legend** that says if you take just one sip from the Nile, you will be sure to come back for another visit.

GLOSSARY

ancient (AYN-chent) Very old or from a long time ago.

artificial (ar-tih-FISH-ul) Not coming from nature, but made by human beings.

climate (KLY-mit) The kind of weather a certain area has.

conquered (KON-kerd) To have taken control of land by winning a war.

drought (DROWT) A long period of dry weather with little or no rain.

Fahrenheit (FEHR-un-hyt) A kind of temperature scale that measures the freezing point of water as 32 degrees (0° C) and the boiling point as 212 degrees (100° C).

highlands (HY-lindz) Areas with many hills or mountains.

historian (hih-STOR-ee-un) Someone who studies history.

irrigation (ih-rih-GAY-shun) To carry water to land through ditches or pipes.

legend (LEH-jend) A story passed down through the years that many people believe.

limestone (LYM-stohn) A rock that is formed from shells and skeletons.

minerals (MIH-ner-ulz) Natural ingredients from Earth's soil that come from the ground and are not plants, animals, or other living things.

origin (OR-ih-jin) The place where something comes from.

pyramids (PEER-uh-midz) Large stone structures with square bottoms and triangular sides that meet at a point on top.

tributaries (TRIHB-yoo-tehr-eez) Small streams or rivers that flow into a large body of water.

worshiped (WUR-shipt) To have paid a great honor and respect to something or someone.

INDEX

B
Blue Nile, 6, 9

C
crops, 13, 17, 21

D
desert, 5, 10

H
Herodotus, 22

F
flood, 13, 14, 17

H
Hapi, 18
highlands, 6, 9

I
irrigation, 17

L
legend, 22

M
Menes, King, 14
minerals, 13

P
Páez, Pedro, 9
pyramids, 18

R
rainfall, 10
rapids, 13

S
scientists, 5
Stanley, Sir Henry Morton, 9

W
waterfalls, 13
White Nile, 6, 9

WEB SITES

To find out more about the Nile, check out these Web sites:
http://www.clpgh.org/cmnh/tours/egypt/natural.html
http://www.website1.com/odyssey/week1/nile.html